9/10/84

CHARLIE & XANE

So in peace...

Sm CAPO

Coping with grief

HEALING LIFE'S GREAT HURTS

By SID CATO

Copyright © 1983 Sid Cato

Parts I and II of this book appeared previously in the Sunday Magazine of the Chicago Tribune, *Robert G. Goldsborough, editor.*

DEDICATION

To Sheila, Cyd and Stuart, who are sorely missed. To their brother and sister, Matt and Julie, who survived their own agonies. And to my new wife, Mary Elizabeth, whose kindness, love and compassion in the final analysis are what made this publication happen.

−S. C.

❦ In much wisdom is much grief; and he that increaseth knowledge increaseth sorrow.
—Ecclesiastes 1:18

We are healed by a suffering only by experiencing it to the full.
—Proust
The Sweet Cheat Gone

What I am saying is, let the relative talk, cry or scream if necessary. Let them share and ventilate. The relative has a long time of mourning ahead...the problems of the dead are solved.
—Elisabeth Kübler-Ross
On Death and Dying

I have always believed that God never gives a cross to bear larger than we can carry....Birds sing after a storm. Why shouldn't we? ❦
—Rose Kennedy, as quoted
by Cleveland Amory in Parade

CONTENTS

Introduction 1

Part I
Ten Seconds to Live 4

Part II
Healing a Great Hurt 11

Part III
**What to Do—How to Survive—
  When Trauma Comes** 17

Most of Us Make It 17

"Will You Ever Forget?" 24

Head Injuries Linked to Problems 26

Most Consoling 33

Visiting Their Graves 35

Why You Should Wear Seat Belts 37

Survival Tips 43

INTRODUCTION

The road back from overwhelming grief is arduous, tortuous, and terribly painful.

We speak now about *grieving of any sort* —
- death in the family
- a broken romance
- the painful separations that so often occur in a close relationship
- watching someone die of a brain tumor
- getting fired
- being forced into early retirement
- suffering a disabling or disfiguring accident
- learning that you or someone close to you has a life-threatening disease or ailment
- changing careers because a failing economy has uprooted your industry
- moving a loved one to a nursing home
- discovering your child is using drugs
- being unjustly imprisoned
- having a child born with an incurable disease
- having a child out of wedlock

Some mistakenly view the only grief worth mention as that which occurs at death of a loved one. Sympathy cards abound in card shops, but their creators are just beginning to confront the wide spectrum of grief *that impacts us all*.

Readers are quite likely to react with surprise or disbelief, initially, to the following *obvious* observation:

This year, every one of us will grieve. When a loved one dies. A young daughter gets pregnant. A friend or neighbor passes on. A husband or wife has a bad accident, perhaps causing permanent injury. Someone we know or care about suffers a stroke or heart attack. A relative or close acquaintance experiences job abolishment, the new hallmark of this decade. A loyal accounting employee, as the long-awaited retirement date looms ever nearer, gets told, conveniently, that—his job no longer is necessary. A woman, after giving birth, discovers her position, as promised, awaits her return—but the company has parceled out all her responsibilities to others.

Those are the kinds of grief we're talking about. The kind of traumas we all face throughout our lives.

And with which we must learn to cope. □

Part I

TEN SECONDS TO LIVE

Of Sheila, Stuart and Cyd, dead two years but never forgotten. Of the tragedy, swift and terrible. Of injustice. And of the man it haunts.

Sid Cato survived the collision two years ago that killed his wife and the youngest two of his four children. Left alive but haunted, he found himself suffering severe headaches, unable to keep awake while driving for even short periods, and unable to sleep soundly or concentrate on his work. How does a devastated man still his anguish and free his mind? Perhaps by talking about it, by telling the story on paper and mailing it away. Here is that story. It's not pretty, but it's useful: It makes you think hard about loving . . . and driving.

THE STOP-ACTION TECHNIQUE

Terence J. Mahoney is a youngish, bespectacled attorney for the famed Philip H. Corboy and Associates law firm, a firm that specializes in personal injury cases.

It was not long after August 17, 1975—a date to remain ever implanted in my mind—that Terry Mahoney taught me the stop-action technique.

It was, he said, an excellent technique to use in recapitulating details of the collision that took the lives of three of my loved ones. Take the incident frame by frame, he said. Freeze the action second by second in my mind when being questioned by insurance men or in giving depositions to attorneys.

The technique helps crystalize your thoughts. By freezing the events frame by frame, it's possible to study and elaborate on all details of each moment of the fatal crash.

The technique showed that three of the six members of my family—along with our country dog, Barney, a black-and-white mongrel— had only 10 seconds to live as we crossed a narrow rural bridge that warm and sunny August Sunday morning.

Ten seconds to live: I slowed the car as we neared the bridge, moving to the left on the one-lane structure, its wood weathered and free of paint.

The bridge isn't the kind photographers shoot pictures of or that people stop to admire. Nothing about that stretch of Streit Road had anything to call attention to it. It was a road like many others we took at random in returning to the city from our country place near Capron, Boone County, in northern Illinois.

What distinguished such roads for Sheila and me was simply that they possessed a country charm, a rural quiet. Sustained us in our periodic escapes from the nervousness of the city and our demanding occupations. Often, such undistinguished rural roads yielded a memorable photograph—a dilapidated barn nestled in an idyllic setting, perhaps, or a bigger-than-life closeup of wheat ready for harvest.

Nine seconds to live: As we came off the bridge, I began to accelerate. Just as quickly, I noticed a road from my left and tapped the brakes. It appeared to be a T-intersection. When I saw nothing to my left on that road, I moved my foot to the accelerator again. I was puzzled: I had seen that T-intersection somewhere before, but that was a different road and a different day.

Photography was one of the fun pursuits of my stewardess wife and me at our weekend home—a modest farm bungalow we remodeled and later enlarged by two rooms.

We also took long, peaceful walks in our forest—20 acres of wall-to-wall trees, plants, and bushes so thick my children called it "the jungle." They made paths crisscrossing the forest. The paths not only opened up all parts of the acreage to the family but made for added fun when we all joined in playing tag or hide-and-seek, sometimes by moonlight.

It was a place of surcease, to regenerate oneself. "No clients," said one close friend, strolling through newly fallen snow in the still forest one day, "within a million miles."

Eight seconds to live: Suddenly, I saw before me a ribbon of highway—a ribbon of sunlight bathed the roadway crossing my path from left to right. Similar to the ethereal glint of the Sears Tower in the sunlight in a recent photo I had taken.

Our weekend visits to the country place came with increasing regularity. Whenever Sheila wasn't flying or we weren't taking advantage of the free passes that came with her job, we'd head for the country. More and more, we went up on Friday evenings. Two glorious mornings to awaken in the tranquility of the country. And since Sunday mornings usually were filled with church-going, the Friday departure meant we could loaf around the place at least one entire day, Saturday.

My children lived with their mother, my first wife, in a suburban community. The near-weekly trip to pick them up gave Sheila and me 45 minutes alone.

Seven seconds to live: Realizing, now, that we were coming upon a cross highway, I hit the brakes hard—a panic stop. The brakes grabbed for all they were worth.

Our time alone, this early, sun-drenched Friday evening, was an unusually pensive one for Sheila and me, full of reflections on our 4½ years of marriage. We talked of what we had accomplished in our marriage, of where we had been. And of where we were headed. We summarized, verbally tied things up neatly. Reiterated goals: a marriage in which each other, not our respective occupations or friends, took precedence. A marriage where sunsets in all their beauty came before demanding clients or passengers—as often as possible, at least.

It was, in retrospect, the kind of summing up one would do were he or she to foresee life nearing an end—through a fatal disease, for example. Or in the kind of crash that was to tie up Illinois Route 23 for hours while the debris was being cleared.

Six seconds to live: The brakes grabbed and held. The heavy car began to slide on loose gravel on the road, past the spot where a stop sign had stood only hours before. One of some 40 signs removed by four young men from the town of Harvard.

Sheila and I were married after a whirlwind, five-week courtship. A courtship during which she was out of town three of the weekends—two of them to Australia, the other visiting an ex-stewardess friend. She had made a floor-length gown for a charity ball we attended. Our first big date.

So ran the beginning of what would be an all-too-brief life together. It was a pattern that was to prevail throughout the 4½ years—but not during our final weekend together. Throughout that weekend, sunny skies warmed and seemingly becalmed the four of us.

My daughter Julie felt the weekend would be too hectic, since the children were to attend an office picnic with their mother and would thus have to return from the country by noon Sunday. My son Matt had track practice Friday, a meet Saturday. So Julie and Matt didn't come with us.

Five seconds to live: The car continued its slide. Out of the corner of my eye I saw a mammoth object bearing down on us: a huge semi truck loaded with freight. I realized the skid would take us into the truck's very path.

Having only two of my four children that weekend enabled us to devote more time to Cyd and Stuart. The two were unusually close to each other, even for a brother and sister. Perhaps it was in part because neither had reached puberty yet. Or perhaps it was because they had been raped, together, three years earlier near my home in Chicago. Neither, we often thanked God, bore any apparent scars from that incident, either physical or emotional.

Stuart, 13, joined us his last weekend of life (clad so proudly in mod coveralls his mother had purchased for him for the new school year about to begin) in outdoors activities—making a work bench for his father, for one thing, out of a piece of wood and a long log we had cut from our forest. He used countless nails.

And picking berries. That was Stuart's primary activity that weekend—harvesting the last of the berries that grew in such abundance at our place. Blackberries. And red and black raspberries.

He stayed out in the floodlit lawn past my bedtime Saturday evening. I am glad I didn't holler at him the next morning.

Four seconds to live: Reacting to the onrushing danger, I instinctively floored the accelerator. Our only chance: to beat the truck across the intersection!

Sheila did holler at him, though, if only gently. He made raspberry jam for his mother and cooked it in too small a pan, contrary to advice. The syrupy concoction dripped into a gooey mass under the kitchen stove.

Later, on Streit Road, a minute away from death, I encouraged him to work on improving his relations with people. ''You're a high honors student, so I guess we can't ask more there. But if you'd only try to get along better with people, there's no limit to what you could accomplish. Why, you could even become President someday," I said. Stuart looked at me and shook his head gently. "Gee, not me, Dad," he disclaimed. He smiled proudly.

Three seconds to live: The semi driver blared his horn. Sheila, seated in the right rear seat, cried: "Oh, my God, Sid!" Stuart cried, "God, Dad!" turned in his seat slightly to the right and raised his hands to shield himself. Cyd, apparently unaware of the impending crisis, continued to busy herself combing burrs out of Barney's fur.

For Cyd, 14, the last weekend of life was spent exchanging confidences with Sheila, whom all the children respected, admired, and liked. The two did creative projects together, listened to a mystery program on radio. Sheila gave her a pair of her slacks.

On Saturday night, Cyd read poetry from Rod McKuen's "Listen to the Warm" book. "Gee, this is good," she enthused over our favorite poems.

Barney was Cyd's dog when she was at home in the suburbs. Sheila's, though, in the country. Abandoned, the skinny dog had been rescued by us from the country's subzero cold.

Two seconds to live: The sky outside the windows on the passenger side of the car suddenly darkened as the massive truck—now only feet away—loomed nearer, blotting out the sunshine that had brightened our spirits that morning.

We had arisen early that Sunday, had gone for an unusual pair of walks in our beloved forest. Barney trotted ahead of us, stopping from time to time to make sure we were coming. And to bite at the burrs matting his hair.

All four of us had gone to Mass Saturday evening, since the children had to be home early Sunday for their mother's picnic. I washed dishes before going to Mass. The water stopped running as I rinsed the final dish—a bearing gone kaflooey in the pump.

One second to live: The crash had begun—the ear-

shattering, mind-blowing gnashing of metal against metal as the huge semi ploughed into the right rear of the car. Stuart's prized jar of jam, propped up on the seat between us for safekeeping for his mother, shattered, covering the ignition key and dashboard.

Water pump out, so no running water at the cottage and no shower. But the kids needed to bathe before going to the picnic.

"No we don't Dad!" they cajoled. "Yes you do," I insisted. So we left a few minutes early for home.

Death: The sound rent the air, filling my brain. Then: silence. I looked in the back seat. It was gone. Acrid dust filled my nostrils and burned my eyes. Glass clogged my throat and nauseated me. The impact had crumpled the car. Only a steeple of steel remained, shrouding me from death or serious injury.

The metal framework of the right-front door had collapsed into Stuart's head, killing him instantly.

Cyd and Sheila, neither wearing seat belts in the back seat, were thrown from the car into a cornfield. Sheila died instantly. Cyd was pronounced dead in the hospital to which all three bodies were taken.

Barney was buried by rescue workers in the farmer's field where he lay. □

EPILOG: Twenty months and 11 days after the tragedy, on April 28, 1977, a judge in Woodstock dismissed criminal charges against the four confessed sign-stealers. The state, he said, failed to prove beyond a reasonable doubt that absence of the stop sign the four admitted removing from the intersection of Route 23 and Streit Road had caused the deaths of Sheila, Cyd and Stuart Cato.

Part II

HEALING A GREAT HURT

In an earlier story titled "Ten Seconds to Live" (July 10), Sid Cato wrote about the final moments in the lives of his wife and two of his children, who were killed two years ago in a car accident. The story touched a large number of readers, and their reactions have become a story in themselves.

'NOTHING TO LIVE FOR'

I had just finished an hour-long shooting session in an Old Town photographic studio. My answering service said a tearful woman had telephoned.

"Oh, I never thought you'd call me back," were her opening words. "I'm so unhappy. Since my husband died, I don't care if I go on living. I don't think I can make it through another day. I look at my bottle of pills and I think, 'Why not take all of them and end it right now?' I have nothing to live for."

She was in the midst of the living hell known somewhat euphemistically as grieving or mourning. Her husband had died six months earlier of cancer, and her reaction to the loss of a loved one was not unusual.

Since publication of the article describing the deaths of my wife and two of my children, I've learned that grief abounds. It's everywhere. Not only among those who encounter death but those who face separation or divorce or the breakup of a close relationship, those who are falsely imprisoned, those who get fired from their jobs. The initial emotional impact is much the same, and the aftereffects are equally debilitating. You think you'll never make it through the day, though somehow you do.

Response to the article often was painful for me but heartwarming. Many readers saw a bond between their grief and mine. Many wrote letters, expressing thanks for the tranquility the article brought them.

"Thank you," wrote a Chicago woman. "Before reading your article, I had walked around the house aimlessly, depressed. I had played the organ in church that morning, but the momentary sunshine had faded, and I again felt alone. It is good to be reminded that it takes years to heal great hurts. Years and years, and then perhaps never completely. Your article helped me. Many thanks for reaching out."

The responses often were terribly touching, as when I met a giant bear of a photographer. He said he had seen the story, and had wanted to phone but didn't know what to say. At the end of our meeting, he rose, grasped my hand in his huge paws, and clasped it tightly for several long seconds as we communed through tear-filled eyes.

At the store where I buy juice by the case, the young owners called me by my first name at least a dozen times on my next visit after the article was published. Because of it we had become friends.

A woman I met at the National Housewares Show wrote: "It was only when I returned to the office that I learned you were the Sid Cato who had written the very moving article I had read in the Tribune Magazine. I enjoyed meeting and talking with you before I realized who you were. Now that I do know, my condolences and sympathy for the terrible tragedy in your life and my prayers for your strength."

PHOENIX WOMEN PRAY

Prayers. A group of women in Phoenix, Arizona, miles and miles from Chicago, had said prayers for me each day after the accident on August 17, 1975. They were still doing so as recently as mid-September as I prepared this report.

At the housewares show a pretty blond named Elaine sort of circled me at first, finally came up to me, and said, "Well, I guess if you allowed such a story to be published, it's OK to talk to you about it."

A circuit-court judge, an old friend and business associate, saw me a few days after the article appeared. "You son of a gun," he said gently, "you made me cry."

A talent agent said he was unable to finish the story. Others said the same thing. Some said they read it bit by bit. A stewardess who was especially close to my late wife said she put the article in her closet—to be read at some future date when the hurt has subsided more.

A Barrington divorcee, whose 17-year-old son had died a year ago in a traffic accident, described her unusual reaction: "I was really quite overwhelmed, preoccupied almost, with your story. I carried it around with me, read it 20 or 30 times one day, even just before going to sleep at night. I guess I envied your knowing about the last 10 seconds."

An attorney and municipal judge in Osawatomie, Kan., called, then wrote to say he wanted to come to Chicago to talk about his problems.

A public relations woman wrote: "I found your article as difficult to read as it must have been for you to write it, but what a powerful statement about life you have given us. Thank you for sharing such a poignant personal tragedy in such a meaningful way."

A public relations executive I have always found rather stoic penned: "Your Tribune piece yesterday was very poignant . . . and how evocative it must have been to write it. My heart went out to you."

Wally Phillips, the radio personality, was sitting in the locker room of the Mid-Town Tennis Club when I saw him one morning soon after the article had appeared. "I was sitting here feeling sorry for myself," he said, "and then I see you and realize how good I've got it by comparison." We talked before and after his tennis lesson, and he invited me to be interviewed on his WGN radio program about coping with grief.

As a result of that interview, a Lincolnshire woman asked me to phone a woman in Adrian, Michigan, who had cancer of the bone marrow. The cancer victim was an acquaintance of another woman whom my caller had met at the King Tut exhibit in Chicago, and now she was asking me to call this friend of a friend to give her a bit of encouragement.

MOST WERE WOMEN

The majority of those who responded to the article were women, but many men did so, too, and in a variety of ways. The publisher of a weekly Canadian tabloid paper asked me to write about previously unrevealed details of the accident. I declined.

At a wedding reception I attended in Des Plaines, I met the Rev. Garry Scheuer and his wife, Carolyn, who both asked for pointers on how to console the grieving, an important part of their ministry. Later the Rev. Scheuer sent me a warm note of thanks and a copy of a book titled "Good Grief."

A TV producer at an advertising agency suggested I syndicate a five-minute radio program on coping with grief.

A newspaperman, who to some might appear hard-bitten, near the end of a lunch casually asked that I do him a favor: Call a friend, whose husband had died recently of cancer, leaving her and a 6-year-old son.

Some men were quite indirect, perhaps because our society discourages males from being overly emotional. One friend, his corporation's vice president for finance, reacted to the article in his own way. "I checked your story closely," he grumbled. "I didn't find any grammatical errors."

Other responses came in: from an actor's agent, who said she was still mourning the death long ago of a 24-year-old daughter; from a former suburban neighbor, who called to talk about the death years ago of her teenage daughter; from an actress who needed to talk about the death in Thailand of her 19-year-old son.

SORROW HAS POSITIVE SIDE

But even the saddest of sorrows has some positive aspects, such as my new friendship with Doug and Joan McCallum of Romeoville. Joan heard me on the Wally Phillips radio interview, "got goose bumps," as she recalled it, and then got in touch with me to ask me to talk to a church group that tries to help grieving parishioners deal with the trauma of death.

I told the dozen or so persons who came to the meeting that feeling grief didn't mean being crazy, that the strange things experienced by those in grief—such as being unable to think clearly or function at basic tasks like cooking or writing checks—were normal for bereaved persons, that the sufferer should realize that others had been in similar shoes before him (or her).

Not long after, Doug had to console a man whose wife had died unexpectedly, and he gave the man some of the points I had made in my talk. "You can't believe how much my friend was helped by what I said," Doug told me. "I hadn't realized how much of what you said had sunk into my own mind for me to give him that much help."

One of the questions uppermost in a mourning person's mind is how long it will take to begin living again—how long to get over the awful hurt. My answer is that it depends on such factors as the severity of the tragedy, the closeness of the individuals involved, the personality of the survivor. Being able to handle grief, though, does not necessarily mean finally putting it out of your mind or completely getting over it.

President Eisenhower, who lost a son, 4, to scarlet fever, wrote in his book "At Ease" that his son's death was the "greatest disappointment and disaster of my life and the one I have never been able to forget completely." Mrs. Elizabeth Shaw, a Chicago voice teacher, had a son who died 13 weeks after he was born. It took her six months to function again, to "get over her sorrow," as the unknowing might say. But almost 50 years after her child died, Mrs. Shaw, now 81, still "feels," as she puts it, the loss of her infant son.

For my part, I've learned that to cope with the grief that comes from death, one must focus once again—or perhaps for the first time—on life, which, as Martin Gray says in his "Book of Life," is for each of us a "new experience." Then he says: "And from all experiences, sweet or harsh, we must extract some good. There is no event without its meaning for a life. Not a day, not a trial but has its significance, on condition that we do not contemplate them, fascinated and immobilized like a serpent's prey, but use them as a help in going forward." □

Part III

WHAT TO DO—HOW TO SURVIVE— WHEN TRAUMA COMES

Most of Us Make It

Don't misunderstand: Sid Cato by no means is the only person to survive an enormous personal tragedy.

In fact, *most people make it*. It's a rarity if one doesn't—though the grieving person usually is convinced things never are going to be better . . . that the sun never will shine so brightly again, that the birds' songs are stilled forever.

You think your problems are insurmountable?

Newspaper and magazine articles appear regularly about persons with big problems they've overcome. Here are three examples:

Congressman Tony Coelho (D.-Calif.), described by the *Wall Street Journal* as an "upbeat, energetic man with the reflexive optimism of a natural salesman."

The newspaper said he is "a rising star among House Democrats." Among other things, he is House Campaign

Committee Chairman. His job is to raise money to elect Democrats, and ''he's raising more than his predecessors ever did.''

Rep. Coelho wanted not to be a politician, but a priest.

But, in the newspaper's words, *''His world fell apart in a single conversation.''* Medical tests showed he has epilepsy, and Catholic canon law bars ordination of epileptics. He returned home to find that his Portuguese-ancestry parents were ashamed of his disorder. A Portuguese superstition holds that epilepsy is punishment for the sins of an ancestor.

Recalls Congressman Coelho:

''I folded.

''I questioned my God, my religion, my friends. I went down into the gutter. There was only one question: Would I stay there or would I get back up?''

He got back up (with the help of comedian Bob Hope), and went on to run for public office.

* * *

Ex-baseball pitcher Ryne Duren, a country boy ''who could throw a baseball faster than anyone had ever seen.''

Newsweek said Duren ''terrorized (major league) batters with 100-mph pitches.''

Off the field, Duren was ''compiling equally awesome statistics in drunken brawls, blackouts and hangovers,'' the magazine reported.

Seven years after helping the New York Yankees win the 1958 world championship, he was out of baseball and in a mental institution. Now he's a crusader against alcoholism, ''trying to steer young athletes away from the obsessive drinking that ruined his career and almost took his life.''

"I was trying to drink myself to death," the ex-pitcher was quoted as admitting. He tried to commit suicide.

That led to a rehabilitation center that "sobered him up and changed his life." Four years later he was asked to direct a rehabilitation center for alcoholics.

Now he's with a firm that helps professional and college athletes deal with drug and drinking problems.

His old baseball team honored him with the Yankee Family Award in appreciation of his work.

Quoted the magazine:

"It's hard to believe that baseball finally is recognizing somebody who's doing something in the field of alcoholism."

He, too, is a survivor.

* * *

Cincinnati homebuilder Patrick Crilley, written up by the *Wall Street Journal* in an article about the "New Generation of Home Builders (That) Profits From Backgrounds in Business and Finance."

Mr. Crilley is a lawyer

It can be slow and insidious, a lingering illness, for example, that turns those of us who ostensibly are well into "walking wounded"—suffering terrible trauma deep within over the pending death of someone we love or care deeply about.

Or it can happen in a flash, as my life changed. One moment a happy family existed—a Boston-born stewardess wife; two lively, challenging teenage children by my first marriage, and a mongrel black-and-white dog, Barney, whom we had rescued the previous winter from the icy cold in the country.

The next moment, I alone remained, saved by a steeple of steel.

who spent eight years with a savings and loan association as its authority on construction lending and financing.

He set up his own company just as the housing recession was beginning.

Not only did the bad economy—"worst housing slump since World War II," the Journal said—make things difficult for homebuilders like Crilley. But, in the newspaper's words:

Mr. Crilley considers himself lucky just to be alive. In an accident two years ago, a bulldozer caught him against a tree and almost cut him in two. He had seven major operations. During his nine-month recovery, his wife ran the business.

"If you can survive the worst economy in decades—and a life-threatening accident—and come out making money like we are, you're a survivor," said Mr. Crilley.

There are lots of them out there—most of us, in fact. ◻

You've read "Ten Seconds to Live" and "Healing a Great Hurt," presumably, before getting this far. After publication of the first article, several friends asked, "How could you possibly write something that personal?" assuming erroneously that it was penned near the time of publication—July 1977.

But it wasn't. It was written when I was paralyzed emotionally. When headaches and nausea prevented me from working or concentrating. When I cried constantly. When I could barely keep awake long enough to drive a car, let alone sit at a typewriter and compose something so painful, yet so moving. It was written during November

1975, little more than two months after what today we call "the accident."

HOW IT CAME ABOUT

During the second week in October—approximately eight weeks after the accident—I attended a luncheon in Chicago of public relations professionals. I went around the table, in my paralyzed but euphoric state, shaking hands and introducing myself.

One man told me his name. I was seated before I realized he had been my best man when I was first married. I had not recognized him, in my condition. An ex-Jesuit priest who had lost a lot of weight, he suggested we have lunch the following week. We did. It was obvious to everyone except me, I'm sure, that I was in a terrible emotional condition.

"You really need to get away," he suggested. *"Take a trip somewhere for a month or so. I think you need it, Sid. Your client will understand."*

Indeed my client did. I had managed to hold on to a California-headquartered computer company whose president was an old business colleague. I'll tell you later about my trips to serve him during September. But he and his wife joined in urging me to get away from things—to take a leave of absence. They kindly insisted my retainer be continued, or I would have been without income.

I packed my car and took off on a month-long motor trip, my alternative to spending time in a mental institution, I believe. As I meandered, alone and lonely, down the highways of Michigan and Indiana and Ohio and West Virginia and North Carolina and Georgia and Florida, I realized that my healing couldn't take place completely until I was able to get the precise facts of the accident out of my mind.

I knew there would be a criminal trial of the four sign-stealers, and I knew I would have to be accurate in my testimony.

How, I agonized, can I hope to heal emotionally if I have to remember all the details of the accident?

"I'll put it down on paper," I recall thinking to myself—in my head, as my wife Mary would say. I would write it as the late Rod Serling, whom I greatly admired, would have: in a dramatic form. I remembered various Serling television programs; I hit on the "countdown" format. I would write the final weekend as I recalled it, with emphasis on the personalities of my wife and two young children, then recap the final 10 seconds—but starting with the point of impact with the truck and going up 10 seconds in time. Then I'd reverse the 10 seconds to form a countdown, and insert them to break up the text. So the story was written when I could barely function, let alone work and think.

I couldn't honestly testify in a court of law that I actually wrote "Ten Seconds to Live," though I have the final edited version somewhere at home. I found some of the words in the published article alien to me. My editor at the *Chicago Tribune,* Robert G. Goldsborough, said he had heard many writers say similar things— that "the story seemed to write itself." That was indeed true in my case.

I do recall wanting to retype it while on the car trip. Of a motel somewhere in the South, I know not where, I remember but two facts:

■ Only two rooms in the motel were occupied: mine and the one next door. (I know because the other occupant made a lot of noise.)

■ And the electricity was out, so I borrowed a flashlight—which I held painfully, and uncomfortably, between my teeth as I retyped the story on my robin's egg-blue Royal portable, given me by a small-town newspaper publisher when I went away to college.

The story that resulted—"Ten Seconds to Live"—was to be nominated as the newspaper's best magazine article of the year, and to draw one of the biggest reactions in the newspaper's history. So the editor assigned me to write a sequel—on response to the original story. It outdrew the original!

"Ten Seconds to Live" in its rough form proved invaluable when friends and relatives gingerly asked for details about the accident. My response, simply, was to hand them the then-unpublished manuscript and walk out of the room.

By May 1977, the traumatic criminal trial of the four admitted sign-stealers was over, the judge having dismissed charges against them because he said the state's attorney, among other things, hadn't shown "that Mr. Cato would have stopped even if there had been a stop sign." Without even attempting to check out my driving record since age 16.

I testified about details of the accident through a veil of tears. The judge asked impatiently several times if I needed a break to compose myself.

'HOW DID YOU RECALL?'

The very Christian Mr. Goldsborough and I had begun playing tennis, largely I know now as therapy for me. We played about once a week or so. He beat me regularly. He and his wife had taken a trip to Europe, and we agreed that I would phone him on his return to set up our next tennis date.

"Before we talk about tennis," his opening words were, *"I just want you to know how upset I am at what the judge did."* He explained that his secretary had placed newspaper clippings about the judge's action on his desk.

"One thing the judge said," he continued, *"I wonder about: that he couldn't believe how precisely you recalled details of the accident. How **did** you remember everything so precisely, almost two years later?"*

"That's easy," I answered. I told him of my dilemma as I drove down Southern highways soon after the accident, and of having written down all the facts so my mind could begin healing.

"I don't understand why you didn't introduce your story in

court," he responded. *I explained that my attorney's advice was not to open myself to questioning about the article. Besides, it was never intended for publication.*

"I'd like to see it," he said, "if you have a copy."

Indeed I had a copy. I gave it to him a couple of weeks later. A few weeks after that I asked what he thought of the story, revealing that it was my only copy. He sounded agitated: "Your only copy! You shouldn't have given me your only copy. What if we lost it!" He insisted on copying it and sending the original back to me.

A couple of weeks later, he asked that I come in to discuss the story. The *Chicago Tribune* Sunday Magazine, he said, would like to publish it. I gave permission, and at the Tribune's direction wrote an epilog.

* * * * *

MILESTONES IN MY HEALING

Milestones I remember vividly that may help others in their healing:

In the hospital—after the accident: I lay—in pain and shock and overwhelming sorrow and loneliness—in a stark hospital room in

---

'Will You Ever Forget?'

My wife asked one especially sorrowful day: "Do you think you'll ever forget?"

Forget "my accident," and the loss of three loved ones.

Forget?

Does one ever forget, ever "get over" his childhood?

The pain of a tragedy lessens each passing day. The memories remain, but amidst fewer tears and less sadness.

It doesn't happen very fast, though. Not in my case, at least. □

a tiny Illinois town. I could see the hot mid-August day outside. I suppose it was a combination of things, including the small amount of drugs I had been injected with, as well as all the excitement of the last few hours: having bits of the windshield in my throat make me gag . . . suffering cuts to my forehead . . . seeing the right leg of my blue jeans pockmarked as if strafed by machine-gun bullets . . . coming close to losing my left eye. A doctor later told me: It was within a sixty-fourth of an inch. Blood from the gash poured down my face at the accident scene and onto my clothes.

(People later would look at the vivid red scars on my right wrist and ask if I had tried to kill myself.)

In the hospital, I was euphoric. I felt a high that must be akin to how one feels when going to heaven. I knew God had immense things in store for me.

I awaited His summons. I complained later to my tax man that the call never came.

"Maybe this is it: the help you're giving others who are suffering," he responded.

During the funeral: One of my wife's pallbearers had his own grief to cope with: His young son had been killed in a traffic accident just a few years earlier, and he and his wife were still getting over it. A big man, he gave some unsolicited advice: "Don't sign your name to any papers for the first month. You'll be pretty punchy."

I was out of it for months. When I later chided him on his faulty timetable, he replied: "I couldn't tell you you'd be funny for months afterward, could I? You'd have been devastated."

Immediately after the accident: I had a two-year-old public relations business that I would have described as doing quite well for a fledgling enterprise. I had clients in Chicago, St. Louis and Los Angeles for whom I produced annual reports to shareholders, and I had six additional pieces of business I had bid on and about which I awaited good news. All but the Los Angeles client quickly faded away—whether because they saw I had a lengthy period of healing ahead of me, or because (as I was convinced at the time) they found distasteful the "smell of death."

Regardless, I ended up with but one client.

I was hampered in my healing by working out of my home. So there was no office or shop to go to, no buddies to help me forget.

Ten days after the accident: My California client and friend, Ryal Poppa, invited me to come out to do some work for the company. I'm sure he was more aware than I of the low state of my emotions. I barely dragged myself through three days there. And then I had to rush back to Illinois for the coroner's inquest into the accident that took three lives.

What stands out in my memory of that visit to Los Angeles was the kindness of an executive recruiter who had placed me in my last corporate position. We had become friends. When he learned I was coming to town, he insisted on meeting my airplane and shepherding

---

Head Injuries Linked to Problems

Sid Cato assumed he was the first ever to suffer the kinds of problems he experienced after his tragic accident: inability to concentrate, lack of energy, forgetfulness, severe headaches.

Under those circumstances, it's easy to question one's sanity.

But recent medical studies provide an encouraging explanation.

The Wall Street Journal, in a Page 1 article, said "physicians often fail to recognize head injuries . . ." which the newspaper said specialists have come to call the "silent epidemic."

The newspaper cited the example of a woman struck on

me around. When it came evening, I confessed I didn't look forward to sleeping alone in a strange hotel room. He offered to sleep on the floor. I declined, but with heart-felt thanks at his compassion.

When I got back to Chicago: I ran. I ran from morning till night. I consumed upwards of a bottle of wine every day. I engaged in a frenetic round of activities designed to keep me from remembering . . . from being alone.

The first year after the accident, I never spent an entire evening alone in our now-lonely apartment. I made sure of that.

About a month after the accident: My former secretary, Patti Kirk, and her husband invited me to join them for a frantic day—we played tennis, showered, read the Sunday newspaper, drank bloody marys, had brunch, meandered through some antique shops, went to a hockey game and then dancing.

I began taking tennis lessons: I don't think I'll ever be a very

---

the head by a falling cabinet. She never lost consciousness, suffered no broken bones or cuts, and was released from a hospital emergency room after a few hours of observation.

"But she didn't get better quickly," said the newspaper. "Constant 'heavy duty' headaches set in, eyesight problems prevented her from driving a car, she tired easily" and she experienced problems in remembering—"such as when she had last bathed or fed" her year-old child.

"It was six months before she returned to work full-time, even longer before her difficulties disappeared."

Throughout all this, the injured woman, 30 years old, didn't know "a lot of the time . . . if I was sick or crazy."

The newspaper reported on studies by schools as di-

good player, but the new, enforced physical activity provided a much-needed outlet—both for my energies and for the time on my hands now that I was a widower. I recall days when I had sunk to the pits of depression. I had nothing to do, nowhere to go. I took my tennis racquet and went to the club I had joined, and hit balls from a machine for an hour. That, plus playing anyone kind enough, *were keys to my making it.*

Little more than two months after my trauma: I left on what would become a 5,500-mile motor trip. I found myself unable to stay awake long enough to drive out of town without pulling over to take a nap.

---

verse as George Washington University and the University of Virginia. The latter followed hundreds of persons who had suffered head injuries that required hospitalization of *two days or less* and whose neurological exams upon release were "completely normal."

Yet, three months later...

. . . 79% said they had headaches

. . . 59% had memory problems

. . . 34% hadn't returned to their jobs

The Virginia researchers also followed up on 159 persons who had sustained "moderate" head injuries involving hospitalization of two to 10 days. After three months, this group's experience was even worse:

. . . 93% still suffered headaches

. . . 90% had memory losses

. . . fully two-thirds were jobless

An assistant professor of neurosurgery at Virginia reported that members of both

For months—at least 12, if not more—after the accident: I cried throughout every lunch, usually with hard-boiled (acting) businessmen. Their understanding exceeded expectations. They weren't the tough guys we're led to believe men are.

My first Christmas: It occurred to me, as I drove alone throughout the South and Southeast on my "getaway" trip: What better place to try to get through the holidays than a place abnormal for a person born and raised in the snow-covered Midwest. The perfect choice was Hollywood, Florida, home of my friends, Pat and Floyd Fulle. (He would become our best man when I remarried, three years later.) I sat by their swimming pool on Christmas Day in 70-degree temperatures, reading a book and trying to forget my troubles. I talked to my two surviving children, who were in Cleveland with their mother, my first wife, at their grandparents' home.

Winter after the accident: Because my late wife was an airline

---

groups complained of rapid physical and mental fatigue, difficulties in doing mathematical work and shortened attention spans.

Other head-injured persons experienced wandering attention, disconnected thought and impulsive behavior.

Said the director of medical-psychology training at the University of Alabama:

"A lot of people . . . are hurting and can't get anyone to believe them. Under those circumstances, so-called mental ills can easily follow the physical ones."

Fortunately, as the newspaper headline proclaimed: "Head Injuries Get More Attention in Medical Circles."

Providing comfort and hope for at least one group of persons suffering from grief. □

stewardess, I was granted unlimited air travel for a year after her death. I used it to visit friends in such places as Boca Raton, Florida. We played tennis (I not very well, I'm afraid), caught Sammy Davis, Jr., in a nightclub in Miami Beach, and swam. I still cried frequently, and agonized over where my life was headed.

I resented violently that God had taken me from being a happily married man and, in one tragic moment, had made me a bachelor— subjecting me again to all the problems of dating. At age 42.

Friends would say, "Your loved ones are happy in heaven with God." "Then why," I asked, "shouldn't I join them?" Suicide, for the grief-stricken, has to be an option debated, however fleetingly.

Redecorating: I acquired, with two other men, the apartment I had lived in for five years, along with the rest of the building. We got it for a low price, and had an attorney make the building a condominium. Each of us bought his floor, and we sold off the fourth floor to another man. I couldn't decide if I should stay where my late wife and I had lived so long. Friends advised both ways: Some said I should move, others encouraged me to stay. I decided that I'd force the issue. If I didn't feel strongly enough about the apartment to redecorate, then I was fated to move. The redecorating felt right. For me, it was part of the vital healing process. It kept my mind off my troubles. It was a small, hesitant step toward becoming a functioning member of society again. But that was to take more than three additional years!

February or March of 1976: I was invited to spend several days at the home of the vice president for safety of a company I had worked for for 10 years. He had been a pallbearer at my wife's funeral. We went up in the mountains of Arizona to take pictures, swam in his swimming pool, sunned—and ate lots of good food fixed by his gentle wife. I took several recipes home with me.

I met a grief-stricken widow in Phoenix whose artist husband had been a close friend. He died of a heart attack while driving his car.

She was in obvious agony. Her face bore the anguish of the bereaved, as I know mine did. (I looked so awful that friends asked if I was taking drugs.)

"How long does it take (to heal), Sid?" she pleaded.

"About six months," I replied.

"That's how long your wife and children have been dead," she said. *"So you're getting better, right?"*

I allowed as how I was. Little did I know.

BECOMING AN ACTOR

I became an actor: In April of 1976, I auditioned for a play to be performed at a neighborhood amateur theater a block from my apartment. I was surprised at being offered an important role. Rehearsals began late in the evening, and continued sometimes well after midnight. They lasted 10 weeks, and the play ran another 10 weeks. I was exhausted by the labor—and overwhelmed, in my condition, by the challenge.

I found myself experiencing a strange sensation: I would awaken in the morning full of pep, only to go downhill rapidly in less than a couple of hours. I called a psychiatrist. He expressed little surprise at my call: "I'm only surprised, frankly, it took you so long to phone," he said. He had read of my accident *nine months earlier*. I told him what I was experiencing: an inability to keep up my energy, to stay awake. "You're suffering from a classic case of clinical depression," he responded without hesitation. "Of course," I said. "Why didn't I think of that!" He prescribed medication designed to help relieve depression in something like 18½ days, which has always struck me as a strange period of time (why not 14 or 21 days?).

The next morning, I was awakened by our longtime housekeeper, who came for her weekly cleaning of the apartment, which she continued after my wife's death.

"What's wrong with you?" she asked.

"I don't know," I said. "I just can't wake up."
"Have you been taking drugs?" she asked.
"Just something the doctor prescribed," I said.
"You better call him," she urged. I did.
"We're going to cure your depression and give you a heart attack," he said nervously.

He monitored my condition throughout the day and then altered the medication. It worked just short of the period he predicted.

I acted in the play until the fall, garnering good reviews—despite the anti-depression medication that made my mouth dry and my body tired. It was an ideal healing process: a new, "play-acting" activity which, along with tennis, kept my mind off the problems at hand. *I was in no hurry to deal with them.*

Throughout these trying times, I was aware that above all, I had to "buy time," to do anything that would put distance between me and my great hurt.

Thereafter: The ensuing months are pretty much a jumble of overwhelming emotions. I had a succession of unsuccessful relationships (not surprising, in retrospect) with a procession of "members of the opposite sex" recommended by well-meaning friends. Women and I did not get on well.

Until, that is, I lucked out (read, "God intervened" if you're religious) two weeks before Christmas 1976—and began a becalming relationship with the woman, Mary Elizabeth Brown-Ryan, who *two years later to the day* would become my new wife.

She would encourage me as I struggled mightily to make a living in a new career, the talent business:

■ Posing for ads, brochures, a vitamin pill package, even an inexpensive type of TV commercial, where a series of still photographs is animated.

■ Doing "voice-overs"—the off-camera narration for industrial films.

- Demonstrating the safety of Volvos at an auto show, the sharpness of the Sunbeam Groomer Razor ("stands whiskers up and shaves them off, at or below the skin line"), the professionalism of Interstate United's industrial food service.
- Performing on camera—for a studio making an industrial film on safety, as I recall, for McDonald's.
- Even doing a TV commercial for a Chicago *radio* station, and man-in-the-street radio interviews for a candidate seeking re-election as Mayor of Chicago.

My new career had lots of glamour, and it forced me to get out every day and "make rounds"—acquaint producers, directors and photographers as well as 11 talent agencies with my capabilities. Every day saw me go deeper in debt. But at least I was working—and taking the first, hesitant, painful steps on the road to recovery.

Eighteen months after the accident— in the spring of 1977: I recall sitting in an attorney's office and interrupting the conversation.

Most Consoling

The single most consoling thing—above all others—during my most trying moments ... was people saying, *"I share a bit of your grief."* That was more comforting than the unknowing can realize—the knowledge that others were helping deflect or dissipate some of my pain.

The second most consoling thing involved *touching*.

All of us from time to time suffer from "skin hunger," as it's called—the need to touch and be touched by another.

I felt that especially after my loss.

It was almost overwhelming. □

"This," I said softly, "is the first conversation with a lawyer I've understood since the accident." Up to that time, my mind was completely befogged around lawyers. When attempting to concentrate, my head would ache, my mind would "close up" and I'd hear talk directed at me only as distant voices.

I remember little about the rest of 1977. Except the awful trial of the four sign-stealers in April—and that my frantic pace slowed somewhat under the becalming hand of my wife-to-be. We took up running, after her repeated attempts to convince me it would be fun. Running became my salvation when depression set in or loneliness occurred. I, who had never run a block before without stopping, now ran a mile, five miles, 8.9 and more than 12 miles in races. Even, eventually, all but the last three miles of a 26.2-mile marathon.

The Chicago Tribune articles: After they appeared in the summer and fall of 1977, I was asked to speak to various organizations:
- a college class concerned with death and dying
- an old-folks' home (as it's referred to; there must be a better term)
- a church group celebrating Family Night

WETTING THE BED

The Family Night talk must have been during the latter part of 1977. I have several beliefs concerning those suffering grief, which I expressed. For one thing, we all fear we're a little crazy (and perhaps we are) . . . we all are convinced that what we're experiencing has never before impacted anyone so severely, and never will be so severe to any poor soul ever again.

I'm convinced that it's beneficial to the grieving to know that (1) what they're experiencing is normal, (2) they're not crazy and (3) they'll someday be able to cope with their grief.

But it takes time, it takes time.

So I told the Family Night crowd of some of my post-accident feelings and experiences, among them that I had wet the bed on two occasions immediately after the accident. I told the audience that a woman friend of my late wife was surprised when I mentioned having done that—because she had had the same nocturnal problem, and wondered if it could possibly be related to the death of her dear friend. Obviously it was.

I liken bed-wetting to a regression to childhood, a cry for someone to please help. In line with that theory of regression, I found myself getting satisfaction from eating meals with my fingers, rather than with knives and forks.

Visiting Their Graves

It's embarrassing to admit: I can't bring myself—not yet—to visit my children's graves.

My wife was buried in New England, near where her parents summer each year, so there's no problem there. I don't get to New England, and her family is close by.

Cyd's and Stuart's graves are quite another matter.

Maybe the pain and sorrow someday, mercifully, will pass. Until that time, I can't *waste* a day—I know that sounds cruel, but that's how I feel—by visiting their graves, and then crying so hard the rest of the day is wiped out for me.

I suppose it's akin to folks who say they don't have to go to church to worship—some of us accept that, and others don't.

I've never heard of anyone else who can't bring himself to visit the graves of deceased loved ones.

But I can't, all these years later.

Writing these words hurts almost as much as visiting their graves. □

After the Family Night talk, a woman and her daughter came forward shyly to admit that they, too, had wet the bed—on the death of their husband and father. They were ashamed to tell anyone about their accidents, and wondered if they were becoming strange, or if it could possibly be related to the death of their loved one.

I also told the Family Night audience that we fill the void caused by death of loved ones with *material possessions*—buying things. I bought a new stereo, new car, clothes I would never wear. Afterward a priest came up to confess that he had done the same thing after a close relative died—"but I never suspected it was linked to her death." He had purchased a gigantic stereo outfit—with no place to put it.

THE FOUR STAGES WE EXPERIENCE

Experts are pretty much agreed that there are four stages in the healing process: denial, anger, bargaining and acceptance.

Some memorable incidents that happened to me illustrate those four phases:

Denial. A subtle form of denial came when my telephone-answering service would say, "Your son called." Obviously, if one son died in the car crash, then the son calling was the surviving son. Yet, I would ask if my son had left his name—to be sure "which son" had called. Also, not facing up to my growing financial plight was another form of denial, though that may have had something to do with the head injuries I suffered in the car crash. (See related sidebar.)

Anger. Everyone who experiences extreme grief finds himself or herself angry—angry at God for *allowing this to happen to me* ("How could you, God?") . . . angry at the loved one for dying. That may sound somewhat humorous at first reading, but my wife and I have a good friend whose father died unexpectedly. She admits to being angry at his leaving problems in their relationship unresolved.

Bargaining. I suspect this stage occurs most often in someone with a terminal illness such as cancer. *"I'll devote my entire life to you, God, if you'll let me live."* That's typical of the bargaining stage. I recall my bargaining as being limited pretty much to a silent promise to be a better person, and to help others, if God would help me through my anguish.

Acceptance. I gained a great deal of solace from Dr. Elisabeth Kübler-Ross' writings, especially her *On Death and Dying**. In one of her books I recall reading—and being startled by —her phrase —

"Life Is Terminal"

That was a revelation to me. "Well, of course life's terminal," one young friend responded not long ago. He, then, has truly faced

---

*Prentice-Hall, Inc., Englewood Cliffs, NJ; 181 pages

Why You Should Wear Seat Belts

I've long been an advocate of using seat belts in my car— ever since I worked for the National Safety Council back in the late '50s. I'm even more so since my auto accident August 17, 1975.

That car crash taught me— if I needed teaching—the *absolute necessity* of using seat belts when you drive.

My stewardess wife and I often wondered if seat belts really work when an accident happens—because they're relatively loose except, theoretically, in a panic, full-brake stop. Let me assure you, THEY WORK! Or I wouldn't be alive, and whole, to tell about it today.

As it was, wearing my seat belt caused my midsection to be sorely bruised. Indeed, one doctor incorrectly surmised that I had suffered "extensive internal damage." He was wrong. I just had lots of bruises.

But here's what I believe

reality. But most of us—especially younger men and women— have not faced up to the fact that we're all going to die . . . it's just a matter of when. Not *if,* mind you, but when.

In the fall of that year: I was asked to act in what would become my final play: ''Everything in the Garden.''

I played the role of a man both dead and alive, both drunk and sober. I got good reviews again. Learning my lines was agony, still. Remembering them was equally hard.

I continued, consciously, to buy time.

'HOW DID YOU SURVIVE?'

People for years afterward would ask how I survived with little or no income. Easy. First I lived off the proceeds from various insurance policies on my wife's life and sold what little common stock we had accumulated. Then, still unable to face reality—and truly unable to

---

would have happened to me had I not been wearing a seat belt when our accident occurred:

■ **I'd have lost my left eye.** I came within a sixty-fourth of an inch of losing the eye, a doctor told me. I assume I cut over my eye when climbing out of the car through shards of glass that outlined where the windshield had been. At a minimum, not wearing a seat belt would have resulted in my requiring dozens of stitches to close up facial cuts. And probably left me with a lot of permanent scars, regardless.

■ **I'd have bitten my tongue off.** As it was, I bit my tongue severely—but not enough to sever it. I naively asked a doctor if biting off my tongue (even if it could have been sewed back on) in the accident would have impaired my speech. ''You could say

work—I got money by remortgaging my condominium. Then I remortgaged the modest country home my stewardess wife and I had bought, largely on her salary. Finally, in the fall of 1977, I had to sell it. It was another painful severing of the past.

I talked earlier about the executive recruiter who befriended me on my initial visit to Los Angeles 10 days after the accident. His name is Paul Papanek, and he invited Mary and me to visit him for a week. This was January or February of 1978.

I remember the excellent meals he cooked us. But more than that, I remember extensive conversations concerning my going back to work. I protested vigorously, making all kinds of excuses. This went on our entire week there.

When we returned to Chicago, I immediately looked at my check book balance. I was broke. The *denial* stage had persisted up to

---

that, yes," he answered dryly.

- **What's more, I'd be walking around with one leg—my right—missing.** My blue jeans were pockmarked in the accident as though strafed by a machine gun. My right leg was cut and bruised. But at least it wasn't torn off, which I believe would have happened had I shifted in my seat even slightly.

- **Or, most likely: I'd have been killed.** Swept away, along with the other three-quarters of the car.

After the accident, I looked around to see how my wife and daughter had fared in the back seat. There was no back seat anymore.

Seconds after the crash, the semi that hit us—flat out—exploded. Probably because the impact tore off my gasoline tank and the truck dragged it a short distance. So while the major potential cause of a fire may have been removed, had a fire occurred

that time. Finally—finally!—I realized I had no choice but to seek a real job.

I prepared a resumé—if somewhat unenthusiastically. I sent it to every executive recruiter in town, but without success. Few even bothered to respond. I continued to answer executive-wanted newspaper ads. No luck there, either.

Mary and I started shopping at Jewel Food Stores, and buying generic foods. That was a turning point: (1) an indication of finally coming to grips with the reality of my financial plight and (2) my first attempt since the August 17, 1975, accident to try to live within our means.

It had taken nearly two-and-a-half years. But we still weren't out of the woods.

---

in my car, I'd have stood a much better chance of getting out safely than had I not worn a seat belt.

Also, I believe doctors were agreed that the seat belts, by holding me stationary at the point of impact, kept me from hitting my head and suffering a concussion. The seat belt kept me from losing consciousness—and thus enabled me to function at the accident scene.

From a healing standpoint, it was desirable for me to be able to take in and comprehend that my family was dead at the scene of the accident. (Healing, I've been advised, is much more difficult for those who have not been able to see, first-hand, their deceased loved ones.)

One final point for you skeptics out there: If seat belts are so great, you're no doubt saying, why didn't they save the others' lives? Stuart's belt didn't save his life because the

ANOTHER RESUMÉ PREPARED

Again, I remember little about 1978, except that my wife-to-be bought me a subscription to the *Wall Street Journal* — to help get me back into the mainstream of business.

Also in 1978, I began teaching at Columbia College of Chicago, which I would describe as a somewhat free-form commuter school with a heavy minority enrollment. I instructed in public relations. I had students ranging from 18-year-olds fresh out of high school to a shapely grandmother (who got straight A's), wife of a doctor. One of the benefits of this activity was that I had something important to do, a place to go, people who needed my presence. Also, I had faculty teas to attend, and briefings for the instructors. And papers to grade. It got me out in the real world.

Throughout all these months after the accident, I continued to see my two surviving children, to visit them at their respective colleges for Fathers' Weekends and the like, and to be with them on holidays, though the details are blurred. I took out loans to put them through college. Things got pretty hairy at times.

As the year 1978 progressed, I grew more and more aware of the unacceptability of the resumé I had prepared after visiting our friend

---

car roof crumbled into his skull. I don't insist that passengers in the back seat use seat belts. My wife and daughter, then, did not have belts on. But not in every instance, obviously, are belts capable of saving lives — not when a speeding truck, for example, tears away three-quarters of your car.

Under those circumstances, there's little that will save you. ◻

out West. Around year's end, I prepared another resumé—inspired, no doubt, by my impending marriage.

I told my late wife's parents late in October that I was going to remarry. They were happy for me.

"When?" they asked.

"As soon as I get a job," I replied.

I called a few weeks later to tell them we had set the date: December 15, 1978, two years to the day from our first date.

"That's great," they responded. "Then you got a job?"

I admitted I had not. But I had great hope.

Landing a job in my profession, public relations, was to take another half year—until July 1, 1979.

On that date—officially, to me—I began my comeback to the land of the living. To the land of the "normal." A functioning member of society.

Just *47 days shy of four years* after my accident.

I still cry over my accident on a sunny Sunday morning on a picturesque country road in northern Illinois.

I still shudder when driving through a country intersection in a car.

I still think, just about every day, of Sheila, Cyd and Stuart. And of the terrible burden their deaths heaped on their survivors, me included.

I'm still unable to bring myself to visit the children's graves, or my wife's. I'm not sure when I'll be able to.

I still have difficulty in facing reality. Where money's concerned, especially.

But at least I'm far better able to cope with my personal tragedy.

And that's what it's all about, in the final analysis—learning to cope with life's *inevitable traumas.*

Learning to cope with grief. □

Survival Tips

How does a person survive a terrible tragedy?

As noted elsewhere, every griever considers suicide as an option—"however fleetingly." One thing to dissuade anyone from taking that drastic action: Whether you can see it or not, there's almost always *light at the end of the tunnel*. Things almost assuredly will get better. Or certainly become more bearable.

You're not the first to suffer grief, and neither will you be the last, alas.

Most of us have strong enough egos to keep us from removing ourselves from this world, fortunately.

For the religious, suicide is a terrible sin.

For anyone, I submit, it's simply *not an acceptable alternative* to living. I ought to know.

Someday—sooner than you may think—you'll know that ending it all is not really preferable to savoring the sunset, smelling the roses, loving, living.

Specifically, what can help you survive?

1. You've got to *buy time*. That's vital. You've got to take each day one at a time. You've got to *prolong* or *extend* your life any way you can—though I would discourage negative conduct as much as it can be avoided.

In other words, stay away from casual sex, from drinking too much, from squandering money so it heaps another burden on your pile of problems.

2. Do plan for the future. Load your calendar with activities, plans.

3. Take up new interests. Nothing can help more than immersing yourself in learning something new: how to operate a computer (I learned, from scratch; it's exhilarating, and it builds confidence!) . . . how to knit or crochet . . . how to play games like chess or checkers really well . . . how to become a better writer. Go back to school—maybe to get your degree.

4. Sports are the very best medicine. I can't think of a better way to help you make your way back from most forms of grief than through active participation in sports. Studies indicate, for instance, that running (you may call it jogging) can help relieve depression. Indeed, it has more positive benefits than just that—if that's not enough. It can buoy your spirits, get you up and out of the house, expose you to new friends also engaging in a positive activity, improve your health—and probably lengthen your life.

And help you begin to truly appreciate all kinds of weather: the misty fall morning, the gentle afternoon rain, the soft, clean snowfall.

Besides, running costs very little: I prefer the inexpensive Sears running shoes, which sell for under $20. You can get them on sale for about $17 last time I looked. All you need in addition to that is a pair of nylon running shorts, inexpensive T-shirt and socks (and ideally, a paperback book on how to prepare for running so you don't injure yourself).

5. Reach out. Help, compassion, love and understanding abound. You'll be pleasantly surprised at the capacity of others.

6. You've got to get outside yourself. The natural tendency if you're grieving is to feel sorry for yourself . . . for some, indeed, to wallow in self-pity. *"The world ought to feel sorry for me,"* you say to *yourself. But it won't—not to the degree we feel sorry for ourselves. That's just the way it is.*

Several things are wrong with excessive self-pity:
 a) You'll go further and further downhill.
 b) You'll soon find your friends fading away.
 c) You may never heal—or, certainly, healing will take longer.

Presumably, that's not what you want.

■ Get active helping others—that'll put your grief in proper perspective. You think things are bad for you? Just visit or talk to others. There's always someone worse off than you, believe it or not.

■ *Give* of yourself—don't just take.

■ Do allow others to share a bit of your grief. Don't close yourself off to others' *need* to reach out to you, to do for you.

Get out of the house. Don't immerse yourself in watching TV, popping pills or eating junk foods, or in consuming great quantities of beer, wine or liquor. The grief will still be there after you sober up. That, plus a hangover, probably—and a growing liquor bill. Breathe the fresh air, enjoy wild flowers nature has provided us, watch the changing cloud formations, the passage of seasons. Join an exercise class. Improve your photography. Write down your feelings.

On that score: My late wife was a supporter of the "Notes to thyself" concept—writing down your reactions as they occur. If you're like me, you'll be surprised (1) at your writing ability and (2) at just how you felt at a given time—a time of trial, perhaps. Re-reading passages I've penned never ceases to surprise me. Some of what I wrote was pretty good. And most of it was much deeper—had much greater substance — than I would have imagined.

7. Try to be positive. It's tough, but I'm convinced it will help speed your recovery.

8. Keep your sense of humor. Without it, you're lost. The ability to see the light side of your most serious situation is critical to your survival.

9. Don't be afraid, or embarrassed, to cry or be angry. Showing emotion of any sort is a natural part of being a human. You'll be surprised at how able your friends are to tolerate or accept your obvious sorrow. Bottling up your tears isn't the solution, and it probably will impede your recovery.

10. Think about getting involved in activities in conjunction with a church, temple, sect or other organization. My way back was helped no end by becoming both a lector and a commentator at Chicago's Holy Name Cathedral—and I'm not even Catholic! Rehearsals, both at the church and at home . . . the actual performances, sometimes at more than one Mass . . . church dinners of lectors and commentators . . . retirement affairs for priests . . . even coffee and cookies after church, all helped (1) fill up time, (2) take my mind off my troubles, (3) challenge me with a new activity, and (4) introduce me to new people.

■ Also, I'm firmly convinced that an abiding faith in a Supreme Being can be a big asset to recovery, or in the case of a terminal illness especially, *acceptance*.

■ Finally, I believe the road to recovery will be made easier through prayer. I found the Lord's Prayer especially comforting in my darkest days—when I was *positive* there was no light at the end of the tunnel.

But there was.

As there will be for most of us. □